T0012132

THE LITTLE GUIDE TO

BULLSHIT

MIX
Paper | Supporting responsible forestry
FSC® C020056

Published in 2023 by OH!
An Imprint of Welbeck Non-Fiction Limited,
part of Welbeck Publishing Group.
Offices in London – 20 Mortimer Street, London W1T 3JW
and Sydney – Level 17, 207 Kent St, Sydney NSW 2000 Australia
www.welbeckpublishing.com

Compilation text © Welbeck Non-Fiction Limited 2023
Design © Welbeck Non-Fiction Limited 2023

ISBN 978-1-80069-545-0

Written and compiled by: Malcolm Croft
Editorial: Victoria Denne
Project manager: Russell Porter
Design: Ravina Patel
Production: Jess Brisley

A CIP catalogue record for this book is available from the British Library

Printed in China

10 9 8 7 6 5 4 3 2 1

THE LITTLE GUIDE TO

100% PURE

BULLSH*T

GUARANTEED

A CELEBRATION OF
OUTRAGEOUS MISTRUTHS

OH!

CONTENTS

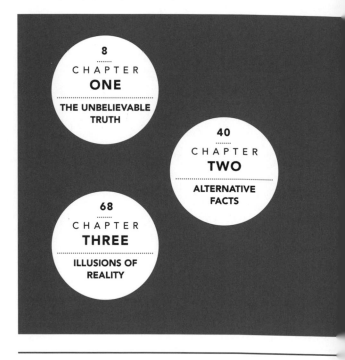

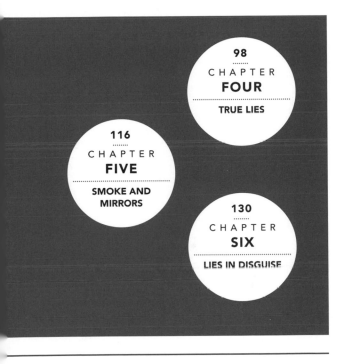

INTRODUCTION

Once upon a time, sex used to make the world go round. Then, it was money. Today, it's bullshit. Bullshit that's bigger, badder, bolder, braver, and more bonkers than ever before.

Look around you; bullshit is everywhere. There's political bullshit, social media bullshit, and office bollocks too. There's bullshit coming at us from all angles, in all shapes, sizes, and smells. We're living in the golden age of nonsense and lies, where misinformation is permitted to be flung far and wide, propped up by cheap lies, propaganda, falsehoods, spin, bias, post-truths, alternative facts, fake news, and all sorts of other malarkey designed to disguise fact from fiction. But, if it stinks so bad, why is it so prevalent, I hear you ask? Because bullshit is big business. Like sex, people buy bullshit. They lap it up.

From Partygate to Brexit, WMDs to that pointless

Zoom meeting you just had, and everything in-between, the bullshit bundle keeps growing and the lies are turning truer every day.

It's time to call bullshit on... bullshit!

The Little Guide to Bullshit is a bunch of bollocks in a nutshell, a timely antidote to help you through the excessive lying, cheating, defrauding, influence, and insincerity that has come to define the 21st century. This tiny tome of trivia is stuffed with delightfully witty snack-sized nuggets of facts, stats, quips, quotes, and wisecracks, each one filled to the brim with fragrant and flagrant BS. Whenever you're feeling frustrated and flustered by fake news, or alienated and alone from alternative facts, or just tired of the lies, simply open this compact compendium of codswallop and laugh at how ridiculous all of it really is.

Just remember to open a window, because this bullshit really stinks.

THE UNBELIEVABLE TRUTH

It's time to put your seatbelt on and prepare for a white-knuckle joyride through lies, damn lies, and statistics that fooled the world.

As renowned bullshitter George W. Bush once said, "Fool me once, shame on you. Fool me, you can't get fooled again" (wonderfully bungling the bullshit at the same time as boasting about it), proving that even the shittiest of bullshitters are the best BS artists.

!!! WARNING !!!
THIS BOOK CONTAINS
BULLSHIT

There is bullshit,
utter bullshit
and *Daily Express*
headlines.

The Guardian

"

The problem with the Internet is everything is true.

"

John Diamond

62
per cent.

The percentage, according to TechJury in 2023 of information on the Internet that is fake.

"

It's all bullshit, folks, and it's bad for ya.

"

George Carlin

"

One of the most salient
features of our culture is
that there is so much bullshit.
Everyone knows this. Each of
us contributes his share.

"

Harry Frankfurt, *On Bullshit*, 2005

Obscurantism.

The practice of deliberately preventing the facts or full details of something from becoming known.

The word bullshit sprang into popularity as British and American slang in 1915 after famed poet T. S. Eliot popularized the term in his bawdy and crude "burn" poem called "The Triumph of Bullshit", which concludes thusly:

And when thyself with silver foot shalt pass

Among the Theories scattered on the grass

Take up my good intentions with the rest

And then for Christ's sake stick them up your ass.

If you smell bullshit at work,
remember to CRAP:

COMPREHEND
- understand that bullshit
is meant to sound appealing

RECOGNIZE
- expect bullshit but learn to
recognize when you hear it

ACT
- confront the bullshit; don't just
accept or disengage from it

PREVENT
- eliminate pointless meetings and
ask to see evidence over opinions

*This CRAP was invented by Ian McCarthy, a researcher
of bullshit** at Simon Fraser University.*

**Not a bullshit job.

“

Money talks, bullshit walks.

”

Stephen King

Bullshitonyms

OBFUSCATION
- the act of making something obscure or unintelligible

MENDACITY
- another way to say untruthful

PERSIFLAGE
- contemptuous mockery

AMPHIGORIC
- meaningless or nonsensical

PREVARICATE
- to speak in an evasive way

EQUIVOCATE
- ambiguous language to conceal the truth

FALLACIOUS
- to deceive or mislead

PERFIDIOUS
- deceitful and untrustworthy

VACUOUS
- showing a lack of thought or intelligence; mindless

HYPERBOLIZE
- represent something as larger than it actually is

Trumpery.

Amazingly, this word dates back to the 1400s, and is another way of saying hornswoggling, or to put a finer point on it - cheating and deception.

No relation to Donald Trump.

"

There are three kinds of falsehoods: lies, damned lies, and statistics.

"

Mark Twain

Cow-slaver.

Cow-slaver is the froth or drool that forms around a cow's mouth as it eats.

In the 18th century it also meant nonsense.

Which makes sense.

66

Hamlet: Do you see yonder cloud that's almost in shape of a camel?

Polonius: By the mass, and 'tis like a camel, indeed.

Hamlet: Methinks it is like a weasel.

Polonius: It is backed like a weasel.

Hamlet: Or like a whale?

99

Hamlet, Act 3, Scene II, William Shakespeare

*"Very like a whale" was popular in the 16th century as a sarcastic response to someone who has said something probably untruthful.

24

Icons of Bullshit: Richard Nixon

I am not a crook.

He may not have been the first world leader to tell a lie, but he was one of the biggest. U.S. President Richard "tricky Dicky" Nixon lied about his involvement in campaign spying and was later exposed in the Watergate hotel scandal. He was forced to resign – the first and only U.S. president ever to do so.

"

A little hyperbole never hurts. People want to believe that something is the biggest and the greatest and the most spectacular. I call it **truthful hyperbole**. It's an innocent form of exaggeration – and a very effective form of promotion.

"

Donald Trump, *The Art of the Deal,* **1987**

66

If it sounds too
good to be true, it's
probably fraud.

99

Ron Weber

If you're only hearing
knowledge from one
source, it's not a fact.
It's an

OPINION.

Bullshit Bingo #1

66

Your call is
important to us.

99

"

Avant-garde is French for bullshit.

"

John Lennon

71
per cent.

The percentage of
U.S. employees who
agree they waste
time every week in
bullshit meetings.

According to a 2014 survey, the average U.S. professional now only spends 45 per cent of their working day doing their actual job.

66

People can come
up with statistics
to prove anything!
'Forfty' percent of all
people know that!

99

Homer Simpson, *The Simpsons*

50 times.*

The number of times less a non-clickbait headline is shared than a clickbait headline.

*In fact, 90 per cent of the online articles we read is because of the headline – not its contents.

Inverting the Pyramid.

Inverting the pyramid is a journalism phrase that relates to an article's story structure: the most important information (the conclusion) traditionally goes first, followed by supporting information and details.

These days, however, clickbait headlines invert the inverted pyramid.

Weasel Words

"

I want to apologize.*

"

Boris Johnson

*This type of non-apology is an example of weasel words, distant qualifiers designed to give an impression something meaningful and specific has been said when the opposite is true, akin to "I'm sorry you feel that way about what I said." #sorrynotsorry

"

Bullshit. Just bullshit, bullshit, bullshit. Full of fucking bullshit.*

"

Shiv Roy, *Succession***, "America Decides"**

*Succession is a masterclass in corporate jargon
bullshit and media manipulation.

"

Look, I tell them that you said
it, they believe that you said it.
They don't really believe you
said it – they know that you never
said it. But it's in their interests
to say you said it – because if
they don't, they're not going to
get what you say tomorrow or
the next day when I decide to tell
them what it is you're saying.

"

Malcolm Tucker, *The Thick of It*

69.2 per cent.

The percentage of statistics you read that are made up on the spot.*

*A statistic gloriously made up by comedian Vic Reeves. Probably on the spot.

100% PURE

BULLSH*T

GUARANTEED

CHAPTER
TWO

ALTERNATIVE FACTS

Everyone's favourite bullshit bingo buzzword – alternative facts – caused worldwide calamity when it first made its political appearance in 2016.

Now, the phrase is effectively applied to anything that sounds like it's been pulled from thin air. The next bunch of bulllshitisms are perfect examples of such...
truthful hyperbole...

66

The only thing standing between you and your goal is the bullshit story you keep telling yourself as to why you can't achieve it.

99

Jordan Belfort, *The Wolf of Wall Street*, 2013

These are our top ten favourite,
and authentic, old-timey synonyms
for bullshit:

1. Balderdash

2. Hogwash

3. Flapdoodle

4. Tommyrot

5. Hooey

6. Twaddle

7. Clatfart

8. Codswallop

9. Flummery

10. Grimgribber

"

The British government has learned
that Saddam Hussein recently
sought significant quantities of
uranium from Africa.

"

**George W. Bush's infamous "16 words" to justify
war in Iraq in his 2003 State of the Union address.
But was it bullshit?**

If you're really successful
at bullshitting, it means you're
not hanging around enough
people smarter than you.

Neil deGrasse Tyson

In a 2022 study by the *Journal of Social and Political Psychology*, it was claimed that right-wing, politically conservative people were more receptive to political bullshit than their liberal counterparts.

The study measured the responses to "statements of political content that intend to persuade voters but are so vague and broad that they are essentially meaningless."

66
I am a fighter and not a quitter.*
99

**Liz Truss, UK Prime Minister
(for 49 days)**

She quit the next day.

Unbelievable Bullshit That's Actually True

1. Humans went to the moon before they put wheels on suitcases.

2. Can openers were invented 48 years after the invention of cans.

3. The job with the highest death rate in the USA is President (at 9%).

4. Malaria has killed half of all people who have ever lived.

5. There's more bacteria in your mouth than in your butt.

6. Woolly mammoths and the Great Pyramids co-existed.

7. Uranus and Neptune have oceans made of diamonds.

> **"**
> I love you is eight
> letters... then again,
> so is bullshit.
> **"**

Ville Valo

> **"**
>
> Whatever you see
> you gotta keep a
> sense of humour;
> you gotta be able
> to smile through
> all the bullshit.
>
>

Tupac Shakur

Bullshit Bingo #2

"

Please hold.
We will be with you
shortly.

"

Brexit Bus BS

> Let's give our NHS the £350 million
> the EU takes every week.*

As part of the Leave campaign for Britain's exit from the EU, in 2016, then Prime Minister Boris Johnson claimed, on the side of a big, red London bus, that the £350m in membership fees the UK sent to the EU would instead be sent to the NHS. This has become one of the most famous lies in British politics.

The Office for National Statistics cited the figure as "wildly overestimated". Johnson continued to use this debunked figure, a clear misuse of official statistics.

How to Detect Bullshit

When it comes to calling out bullshit,
simply remember SHARE.

SOURCE

Rely on official sources for information.

HEADLINE

Always read to the end of an article,
not just the headline.

ANALYSE

Analyse and double-check the facts.

RETOUCH

Images and graphs are often retouched
from the original.

ERROR

Look out for mistakes.

Life is too short
for grief. Or regret.
Or bullshit.

Edward Abbey

The Dunning–Kruger Effect

The more incompetent you are... the smarter you think you are.

This now-famous psychological bias describes, in short, how incompetent people overestimate their own competence to appear more competent.

"

If you can't dazzle them with brilliance, baffle them with bull.

"

W.C. Fields

The first dictionary to include the word "bull" to mean BS was the Oxford English Dictionary of North American slang, published in 1942.

> **We are bullshit.
> You are bullshit.
> I am bullshit.**

Roman Roy, *Succession*, "With Open Eyes"

> **"**
> The only person
> to blame is the
> person making up
> the bullshit.
> **"**

Oliver Sykes

Icons of Bullshit: Boris Johnson

"

Nobody told me that what we were doing was against the rules, and as I said in the House of Commons when I went out into that garden, I thought that I was attending a work event.*

"

Boris Johnson, discussing the events of "Partygate", 2020

He would later became the first Prime Minister to commit a criminal offence in office, while in breach of his own Covid laws, and resign as an MP in 2023.

The act of shoe polishing to a spectacular shine is known as bulling. During WWI, the word "bullshit" became popular among Allied soldiers. British soldiers were ordered by commanding officers to ensure their shoes were always spotlessly shined, despite the muddy and bloody world war that waged around them.

Australian troops would soon mock the pretence as "bullshat", to refer to shoes that had been polished solely for display purposes.

66

You can have your own
opinions, but you can't have
your own facts. Truth is not
a democracy. It doesn't give
a shit what you 'believe'.

99

Ricky Gervais

Bullshit makes you sound **35 per cent** more intelligent.*

"That's bullshit.

Infuriating Bullshit Syndrome.

A common bodily reaction when told an overwhelming level of bullshit is to experience an uneasy feeling in your guts. Don't worry: the feeling passes once the bullshit stops.

"

Above all, don't lie to yourself.
The man who lies to himself and
listens to his own lie comes to a
point that he cannot distinguish
the truth within him, or around
him, and so loses all respect for
himself and for others. And having
no respect he ceases to love.

"

Fyodor Dostoevsky

"

A truth that's told
with bad intent
Beats all the lies
you can invent.

"

William Blake

66

Welcome to the world of bullshit, my dear. You have arrived.

Elton John

100% PURE

BULLSH*T

GUARANTEED

CHAPTER
THREE

ILLUSIONS OF REALITY

We live in a post-truth world, whatever that means. A world where truthiness is the truth, the whole truth, and yet nothing like the truth.

It's an illusion, not rooted in anything as boring as facts and evidence. When it comes to keeping your mind clear from bullshit, you're going to need all the help you can get to detect it.

The wit and wisdom of the next few pages will help keep you properly informed. The more you know, and all that...

66

The reason why there's so much
bullshit I think is that people just talk.
If they don't talk, they don't get paid.
The advertiser wants to gain sales.
The politician wants to gain votes.
And since they don't have anything
really valid to say, they just say
whatever they think will interest the
audience to make it appear they know
what they're talking about. And what
comes out is bullshit.

99

Harry Frankfurt, *On Bullshit*, 2005

Cocktail: The Bullshit

Ladies and gentleman,
The Bullshit cocktail.
Designed to be swallowed in one.

Ingredients

1 shot of Jägermeister
1 shot of Tequila
1 shot of Red Bull

Make It Right

Dump the ingredients
in a glass. Drink.
Regret the decision.*

Yes, it tastes like absolute bullshit.

In a recent
survey conducted by
Harvard University,

75 per cent

of respondents admitted
to telling at least
two lies per day.

According to a recent York University study, these are the ten most-told little white lies we tell our nearest and dearest every day.

1. "I'm five minutes away."

2. "My phone's been acting weird."

3. "Let's just do one more drink."

4. "I'm almost finished."

5. "I've got to run."

6. "Let's hang out soon."

7. "I'll call you later."

8. "I've been totally slammed."

9. "Just kidding!"

10. "I had this in my drafts folder."

"

History is a set of lies agreed upon.

"

Napoleon Bonaparte

66

Ask me no
questions, and I'll
tell you no fibs.

99

Oliver Goldsmith

Great liars are also great magicians.

Adolf Hitler

"
Computer-game
bullshit.
"

**Director Quentin Tarantino describing the
prevalent use of CGI in most modern movies**

The word "bull" to mean nonsense dates back to the 17th century. It derives from the French *bole*, to mean "fraud" and "deceit".

On average, an individual is lied to **50 times** a day, either by businesses, social media, news, colleagues, family, or friends.

Anyone who uses the phrases
**"Trust me, I know what
I am talking about"**,
"To be perfectly honest",
"I swear I'm telling the truth"
and "I promise" are

75 per cent

more likely to lie. Honest people
don't feel the need to convince
you of their honesty.

There are three kinds of lies:

White lies, Serious lies, and *Bullshit*.

1. A little white lie is replying "No" to the question: "Does this dress make me look fat?"

2. Serious lies threaten the foundation of societal functioning.

3. Bullshit is the fifty shades of grey area in between point 1 and point 2.

"

Nazi propaganda specifically denies that such a thing as 'the truth' exists. If the Leader says of such and such an event, 'It never happened' – well, it never happened. If he says that two and two are five, it's five. This prospect frightens me much more than bombs.

"

George Orwell, 1943

Bull-Related Terms

Bulls have long had a bad reputation,
judging by their idioms...

1. Bull-Necked

2. Take The Bull By The Horns

3. A Bull In A China Shop

4. Cock And Bull

5. A Red Rag To A Bull

6. Hit The Bull's-Eye

7. Mess With The Bull (And You) Get The Horns

8. Like A Bull At A Gate

9. As Strong As A Bull

10. As Useful As Tits On A Bull

11. Milk The Bull

12. Seize The Bull By Its/The Horns

66

A half-truth
is the most
cowardly of lies.

99

Mark Twain

I always tell
the truth.
Even when I lie.

Al Pacino

Icons of Bullshit:
Lance Armstrong

The once universally loved professional U.S. cyclist Lance Armstrong won a record-breaking seven Tour De France victories and even defeated cancer. He was a hero.

However, in 2012, after years of denial, it was revealed all to be bullshit. He had been doping the entire time with performance-enhancing drugs. Armstrong was permanently banned from professional cycling.

66

Give them the old Trump bullshit.

99

Donald Trump

Bullshit Business Bingo

The top ten most disliked nuggets of corporate jargon according to *Forbes*.*

1. New normal
2. Quiet quitting
3. Circle back
4. Bleisure
5. Hits different
6. Upskilling
7. Desk bombing
8. Growth hacking
9. Quick wins
10. On mute

*76 per cent of men are more likely to use bullshit jargon than women (66 per cent).

66

Your bait of
falsehood takes this
carp of truth.

99

William Shakespeare

"

We are in a fight and it's a fight not just about alternative facts but it's a fight for the objective truth.

Steven Spielberg

In 2016, the year Donald Trump was elected president and the year Brexit was initiated, was Oxford Dictionary word of the year was...

POST-TRUTH.

Coincidence?

Doubling down on an ***obvious lie*** is a clear sign someone is **bullshitting.**

TLDR.

Too long, didn't read.

*A popular Internet acronym to denote the reading
of a headline to gain the gist of an article but not
the actual facts contained underneath.*

66

Whenever you're exposed to
advertising in this country
you realize all over again that
America's leading industry
is still the manufacture,
distribution, packaging, and
marketing of bullshit.

99

George Carlin

Repeat a lie often enough and it becomes the truth.

Joseph Goebbels

According to the *Washington Post*, at the height of the COVID-19 pandemic, misinformation and disinformation was

six times

more likely to be shared than factually correct evidence.

The Epimenides Paradox

Fifteen hundred years ago, Cretan philosopher Epimenides coined the "Epimenides Paradox", following his statement: "All Cretans are liars."

Epimenides, a Cretan, must be a liar. But if he is a liar, what he says is untrue, and therefore is true. This Liar's Paradox is an example of a phrase that is both true and false at the same time.

It's where bullshit lives.

100% PURE

BULLSH*T

GUARANTEED

CHAPTER
FOUR

TRUE LIES

Bullshit can be squeezed out in all shapes and sizes. It can be soft or hard; dry or wet; chunky or one long tubular bell. It can be a little white lie or a massive delusion of grandeur.

Your job is to pick through the pieces and work out what bullshit matters to you the most. Because at the end of the day, we're all bullshitters.

Bullshit Bingo #3

"

We pride ourselves on our customer happiness.

"

"

Don't be so overly dramatic about it, Chuck. Sean Spicer, our press secretary, gave alternative facts to that.

Donald Trump's advisor Kellyanne Conway's now-infamous reply to White House journalist Chuck Todd, in 2016, regarding Trump's inauguration attendance.

Five.

The number, or more, of lies a prolific liar* will tell per day.

*Prolific liars tend to be younger, male, and have higher occupational statuses and are more likely than the average person to believe that lying is acceptable in some circumstances. They tell 19.1 lies for every one big lie told by an average person.

60 per cent.

The number of adults incapable of having a conversation without lying once every ten minutes.

$$utters_A(p) \land \neg K_A(p) \land \neg K_A(\neg p)$$

According to Martin Caminada's Truth, Lies and Bullshit: Distinguishing Classes of Dishonesty theory, bullshit can be characterized "in its simplest form" as the equation above.

Looks like bullshit to me.

> **“**
>
> # Bullshit baffles brains.
>
> **”**
>
> **Elon Musk**

Truthiness.

It was legendary late-night talk-show host Stephen Colbert who popularized this incredible bullshit word for bullshit in 2005. Colbert also launched "mathiness" for numbers that don't quite add up.

"Truthiness is what you want the facts to be as opposed to what the facts are. What feels like the right answer as opposed to what reality will support."

"

He's trying to tell us he cares about the middle class. Give me a break. That's a bunch of malarkey.*

President Joe Biden being polite about Donald Trump

**Biden's go-to bullshit catchphrase is the folksy "malarkey",
a word that was first used in the 1920s to mean "nonsense",
but its origins remain a mystery.*

Quit yo jibber-jabber!

BA Baracus (Mr T.), *The A Team*

Bloviation.

The most perfect example of onomatopoeia – a word that sounds like its meaning.

To bloviate means to speak long-winded pretentious nonsense, i.e., the worst kind of bullshit.

"

Bullshit is a greater enemy of the truth than lies are.

"

Harry Frankfurt, *On Bullshit*, 2005

Christmas Bullshit

"

I've always wanted
one of these!

"

"

Exaggeration is truth that has lost its temper.

"

Khalil Gibran

In 2022, in the *Journal of Behavioural and Experimental Finance*, a study discovered that those most vulnerable to financial bullshit are young, rich men who are overconfident in their own financial knowledge. So,

85 per cent

of bankers, then.

Bullshit Jobs

In 2018, American anthropologist David Graeber released his seminal book that claimed that 50 per cent of all modern jobs are bullshit jobs. Graeber distilled them into five groups:

1. Flunkies

2. Goons

3. Duct Tapers

4. Box Tickers

5. Taskmasters

Which one is yours?

I've been accused of vulgarity. I say that's bullshit.

Mel Brooks

100% PURE
BULLSH*T
GUARANTEED

CHAPTER
FIVE

SMOKE AND MIRRORS

Deception and disinformation,
boasts and exaggeration,
spin and bias, propaganda and fraud,
or our personal favourite – untruths.

Call it what you want but look a
bit closer under the bonnet and all
you'll smell is freshly baked bullshit;
hogwash designed to fabricate,
obfuscate and bloviate the truth into
submission. Read all about it...
but don't believe a word...

70 per cent.

The percentage of British voters who consider former Prime Minister Boris Johnson a habitual "liar", as well as "incompetent" and "untrustworthy" in a 2022 poll by *The Times*. Only **16 per cent** regarded him in positive terms.

How to Be the Best Bullshit Artist

1. Know nothing

2. Say anything

3. Distort the evidence

4. Speak loudly

5. Ridicule and bully the other side of the argument

6. Refute the premise of a question

7. Answer an unasked question

8. Ignore a question you don't like

9. Say how great you are about everything

10. Pander to your base

Shitlist: Famous Songs About Bullshit

1. "Bullshit" – Grace Jones

2. "Party and Bullshit" – The Notorious B.I.G.

3. "No Bullshit" – Chris Brown

4. "Everything is Bullshit" – Willie Nelson

5. "I C Your Bullshit" – Snoop Dogg

6. "Back on the Bullshyt" – 2 Chainz

7. "The Bullshit Song" – Clay Tallstories

8. "Bullshit" – The Alkaholics

9. "In the Name of Bullshit" – Jonathan Mann

10. "It's a Bullshit" – Subconcious

50 per cent.

The percentage of the time, on average, that people can detect lies.

60
per cent.

The number of
Americans who, in 2023,
believe humans only use
10 percent of their brain.
Come on, people!

> ❝
> I don't have a
> short temper;
> I just have a quick
> reaction to bullshit.
> ❞

Elizabeth Taylor

Deja Moo.

The feeling that you've heard this bullshit before.

*Tommy Cooper's joke.

If you tell the truth, you don't have to remember anything.

Mark Twain

"

I'm not upset
that you lied to me,
I'm upset that
from now on I
can't believe you.

"

Friedrich Nietzsche

66

Never tell a lie
when you can
bullshit your way
through it.

99

Eric Ambler

80
per cent.

According to Statista, this is the percentage of U.S. adults in 2023 who have consumed fake news.

If you think you're being lied to, listen to the words being said. According to the American Psychological Association, bullshitters tend to use

smaller, and fewer,

words than honest people.

100% PURE

BULLSH*T

GUARANTEED

CHAPTER
SIX

LIES IN DISGUISE

The truth is often unbelievable and lies are sold in disguise. Sometimes fiction is stranger than fact, and sometimes statistics and figures don't add up!

The world is full of bullshit artists, scoundrels, cheats, liars, phoneys, and frauds still waiting to be exposed, and now it's time to call them out. Remember, if it sounds too good to be true, it's probably bullshit!

You *can* bullshit a bullshitter.

In 2021, psychologists at the University of Waterloo tested the adage "You can't bullshit a bullshitter" and found that, actually, bullshitters who deliberately say bullshit are more likely to believe, and spread, other people's bullshit.

Develop a built-in bullshit detector.

Ernest Hemingway

61
per cent.

In 2023, the percentage of Americans who believe news on social media contains misinformation, according to the Knight Foundation.

The Guru Effect

The Guru Effect occurs when people assume something must be important if it's difficult to understand.

7 out of 10.

The number of people who claim to use bigger words to impress others at work.

Sesquipedalian.

The name to describe someone that overuses big words to appear smart, even if they don't really know what it was about because they can't understand the words.

66

All we know is that we know nothing.

99

Socrates

Bullshit Receptivity Scale

In 2020, Australian psychologists used data from 10 English-speaking nations, and 40,000 teenagers, to devise a Bullshit Receptivity Scale.

The data concluded that North American boys from higher socioeconomic backgrounds bullshit more than anyone else. That group tended to over-estimate their knowledge and rate themselves higher, more confident, more deserving, and more popular than any other group.

"

Bah! Humbug!

"

Ebenezer Scrooge, created by Charles Dickens,
***A Christmas Carol*, 1843. This famous reference**
declaring Christmas to be a fraud is one of the
oldest written synonyms of bullshit

66

I did not hit her.
It's not true. It's bullshit!
I did not hit her. I did not.
Oh hi, Mark.

The Room, 2003*

This line has gone down in infamy as perhaps the worst acted, scripted and performed line in the history of cinema in what is known as the worst movie of all time.

"

Bullshit is so ubiquitous because humans are social by nature, so if they can get social benefits from saying something, even if it's not true, they will. We're configured mentally by this need to succeed socially.

"

Martin Harry Turpin

66

Bullshitting is defined as language that's meant to impress others without any regard for the truth.

Mane Kara-Yakoubian

Bullshitocracy

In 2015, iconic U.S. comedian Jon Stewart gave a speech about America's ruling "bullshitocracy" as a farewell warning in his final *The Daily Show* episode, concluding with the wonderful line, "If you smell something, say something." Stewart's Bullshitocracy comes in three basic flavours:

1. Making bad things sound like good things.

2. Hiding the bad things under mountains of bullshit.

3. The bullshit of infinite possibility.

66

Bullshit is everywhere.
There is very little that
you will encounter in
life that has not been, in
some way, infused with
bullshit; not all of it bad.

99

Jon Stewart

38 per cent.

In 2019, the share of adults who trusted the media in the UK.

That number fell to *7 per cent* in 2022 following the pandemic.

❝

Apparently people don't like the truth, but I do like it; I like it because it upsets a lot of people. If you show them enough times that their arguments are bullshit, then maybe just once, one of them will say, 'Oh! Wait a minute – I was wrong.' I live for that happening. Rare, I assure you.

❞

Lemmy Kilmister

67
per cent.

In 2022, the number of U.S. citizens who have a great level of confusion caused by fake news about the basic facts of current issues and events.

38.2
per cent.

The percentage of people in the U.S. that had shared fake news on social media in 2020, the year of the U.S. presidential election.

"

Money gives men the power to run the show. It gives men the power to define our values and to define what's sexy and what's feminine – and that's bullshit.

"

Beyoncé Knowles

90
per cent.

The number of total lies told by the average person that represent little white lies.

The remaining *10 per cent* are deemed "serious" lies.

Bullshit Around the World

1. *Quatsch* – German
2. *Connerie* – French
3. *Mierda* – Spanish
4. *Cazzate* – Italian
5. *Onzin* – Dutch
6. *Lort* – Danish
7. *Paskaa* – Finnish
8. *Skitsnack* – Swedish
9. *Głupie gadanie* – Polish
10. *Besteiro* – Portuguese

A lie can travel halfway around the world while the truth is putting on its shoes.

Winston Churchill*

Or was it?

Lying is a craft,
bullshitting is an art.

> 66
>
> I am a firm believer in the people. If given the truth, they can be depended upon to meet any national crisis. The great point is to bring them the real facts, and beer.
>
> 99

Abraham Lincoln

The Bullshit Paradox

The more often a lie is repeated, even in the context of debunking it, the more believable it becomes.

66

There's a lot of things wrong with America, but one of the few things still right with it is that a man can steer clear of the organized bullshit if he really wants to. It's a goddamned luxury, and if I were you, I'd take advantage of it while you can.

99

Hunter S. Thompson

The Bullshit Asymmetry Principle

This principle, also known as Brandolini's Law, states that "The amount of energy needed to refute bullshit is an order of magnitude bigger than to produce it."

Put simply: it's harder to debunk a lie when there's a steep mountain of bullshit to climb.

Four Questions

Smell bullshit? These four expertly devised questions will waft it away:

1. "How do you know what you know?"

2. "Who besides you shares this opinion?"

3. "Explain this in simpler terms I can understand."

4. "What's in it for you?"

"

One man's accuracy is another man's bullshit.

"

Alex Winter

Bullshit We Were Fed As Kids

1. Sugar will make you hyperactive - **it doesn't**

2. You can't swim for an hour after eating - **you can**

3. Cracking your knuckles will give you arthritis
- **it won't**

4. Watching TV too close to the screen will
damage your eyes - **it can't**

5. Eating carrots will help your vision - **it won't**

6. You only use 10 per cent of your brain
- **you'd be dead**

7. You swallow 8 spiders a year - **don't be silly**

8. Vitamin C prevents colds - **it doesn't**

9. Santa's real - **wake up, kid**

10. Shaving your legs makes the hair grow
back thicker - **try it**

"

Dumbe Speaker! that's a Bull.
Thou wert the Bull

Then, in the Play. Would I
had seene thee rore.

"

The Antipodes, a comedie, by Richard Brome.
Performed by the "Queenes Majesties Servants"
at Salisbury Court, Fleet Street, London, 1638.
Possibly one of the first uses of bull in performance.

"

Crosses only scare
vampires away
because they're
allergic to bullshit.

"

Richard Pryor

66

Men occasionally stumble over the truth, but most of them pick themselves up and hurry off as if nothing ever happened.

99

Winston Churchill

You can sprinkle it with sugar all you want.

But if it smells like bullshit and it looks like bullshit –

it's bullshit.

Bullshit is a bullshitter's way of polishing a turd.

A 2022 study in the *Journal of Marketing Communications* revealed that men with beards tell fewer lies than those who were clean-shaven.

37 per cent.

The percentage of people in the UK who believe their job to be bullshit, according to YouGov data.

> **66**
>
> I did not have sexual relations with that woman, Ms Lewinsky.
>
> **99**

(Lie)

In 1988, President Bill Clinton and intern Monica Lewinsky had an affair inside the White House. It was the biggest sex scandal of the century. Famously, Lewinsky gave Clinton a blowjob in the Oval Office, which helped to "manage his anxieties".

70
per cent.

The percentage a person is more likely to lie on a phone call over a face-to-face chat.

"

All of our lives
are governed by a
certain degree of
faith in bullshit.

"

Dan Simmons

It is estimated that people lie somewhere between **two and six times a day.**

Men and women lie
the same amount, but
for different reasons.
On average, men lie to
make themselves look
better whereas women
lie to make the other
person feel better.

On average,
a person will lie
three times
in the first
ten minutes
of meeting
someone new.

6 out of 10.

The number of orgasms that are fake news by women.

"

I'm just not very good at bullshitting.

"

Barack Obama

> ## 66
>
> So, *Back to the Future*'s a bunch of bullshit?
>
> ## 99

Scott Lang, *Avengers Endgame*, 2019

88
per cent.

The percentage of New Year's resolutions – one of life's biggest bullshits we dump on ourselves – that go unfulfilled.

Poppycock.

Dutch for "soft poop"
or *poppekak*.

Bunkum.

Empty, insincere, or foolish talk.

Bunkum originated from 19th-century North Carolina congressman Felix Walker, who represented Buncombe Country. In 1820, Walker made a long-winded speech that was so vacuous it led to the "Missouri Compromise", an agreement that sat on the fence between pro-slavery and anti-slavery factions.

Agnosis.

The active indifference,
avoidance, or ignorance
of knowledge.

> **"**
>
> # I'm tired of this back-slappin' 'Isn't humanity neat' bullshit. We're a virus with shoes.
>
> **"**

Bill Hicks

66

I got Brexit done.

99

Boris Johnson*

It's still not done.

66

This dude is bullshit.

99

Elon Musk, about cryptocurrency founder of FTX, Sam Bankman-Fried, who defrauded clients of $26 billion, the biggest financial fraud in history.

66

Just another bullshit artist.

**Former President Donald Trump,
about Elon Musk**

"

Careful you don't step in the bullshit.

"

Private Jackson, *Saving Private Ryan*, 1998

January is the worst month of the year for telling lies.

This month, Americans tell others more than *seven* **lies per day**, an increase of **50 per cent**.

Look in the mirror:
Bullshit comes from
within. We tell ourselves
two lies a day.

"

Be wary of someone
who has never failed
or seem to have no
faults... Too good to be
true usually is. Perfection
hides something.

"

Henry Cloud

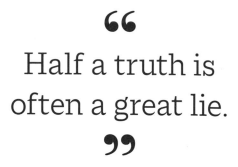

66

Half a truth is often a great lie.

99

Benjamin Franklin

Half the lies you
tell *aren't* true.

> **"**
>
> # The bullshit never ends. That's the main thing to remember. It never ends.
>
> **"**

Sam Lipsyte